My First Book of Garden Bugs

Mike Unwin

Illustrated by
Tony Sanchez

A & C BLACK • LONDON

Published 2009 by A & C Black Publishers Limited
36 Soho Square, London W1D 3QY
www.acblack.com

ISBN: 978-1-4081-1415-5

A CIP catalogue for this book is available from the British Library.

This book is produced using paper that is made from wood grown in managed, sustainable
forests. It is natural, renewable and recyclable. The logging and manufacturing processes
conform to the environmental regulations of the country of origin.

Printed and bound in Singapore by Tien Wah Press (Pte) Ltd.

Also in this series:

RSPB My First Book of Birds by
Sarah Whittley and Mike Unwin, illustrated by Rachel Lockwood.
RSPB My First Book of Garden Wildlife by Mike Unwin, illustrated by Tony Sanchez.

Original concept for **My First Book of Garden Birds** by Rachel Lockwood and Sarah Whittley.

To see our full range of books
visit www.acblack.com

Contents

Minibeast magic

Minibeasts are hopping, buzzing, crawling and wriggling all over your garden. But you might not see them all at once. It helps if you know where to look.

Take a bug's eye look at your lawn. Lots of minibeasts live in the grass or burrow through the soil below. Try lying on your tummy and seeing what you can spot.

Minibeasts can be hard to see among the leaves. Explore the bushes and borders to see what is lurking in the greenery.

Take a peek under rocks and logs. Some minibeasts like the damp and the darkness. Make sure you put them back carefully afterwards.

Keep an eye on the sky. All kinds of minibeasts take to the air as they go about their business. Watch where they land, then sneak up for a closer look.

Are you ready to meet some minibeasts? Read the clues on each Guess who! page and see if you can work out which bug is hiding there.

You'll find the answer on the following page.

How many legs?

There are thousands of different kinds of minibeasts. Each kind belongs to one of several different groups. You can tell the groups apart by counting their legs.

 All insects have six legs.

 All spiders have eight legs.

 Anything with more than eight legs is not a spider or an insect.

 Slugs and snails have no legs at all — just one big foot.

Who is it?

Oh dear! Somebody seems to be stuck in a hole.
Can you see that furry bottom struggling to get out?
Buzz, buzz, buzz! It sounds rather annoyed.

But who is it?

Bumblebee

It's a bumblebee. But she wasn't stuck. She was just visiting her nest. Now she is looking for flowers full of sweet nectar to drink. A female bumblebee sleeps all winter. In spring, she sets out to find a snug place to lay her eggs. An old mouse hole is perfect.

Who is it?

There's an old brown leaf curled up on the stinging nettles. Or is it?

Look closer. Leaves don't have legs.

Could something be hiding there?

Peacock butterfly

A-ha! It's a peacock butterfly.

This insect can be hard to spot. Its folded wings look just like a dead leaf. But what beautiful colours when it opens its wings! Those bold round markings are pretend eyes. They help to scare away hungry birds that might want to eat it.

Who is it?

Yuk! There's something sticky and frothy on the long grass.

It looks like a blob of spit. Look closer. Lots more are scattered about.

What are they?

Froghopper

That froth is called cuckoo spit.
Take a peek inside. You'll find a tiny
insect called a froghopper.
It grows up safely inside the froth,
then crawls out as an adult and
hops away. Just like a miniature frog.

Who is it?

Look closely at these leaves. Something's hiding on the other side, hoping that you won't spot it. Its neat, little body is shaped like a shield.

What do you think it is?

13

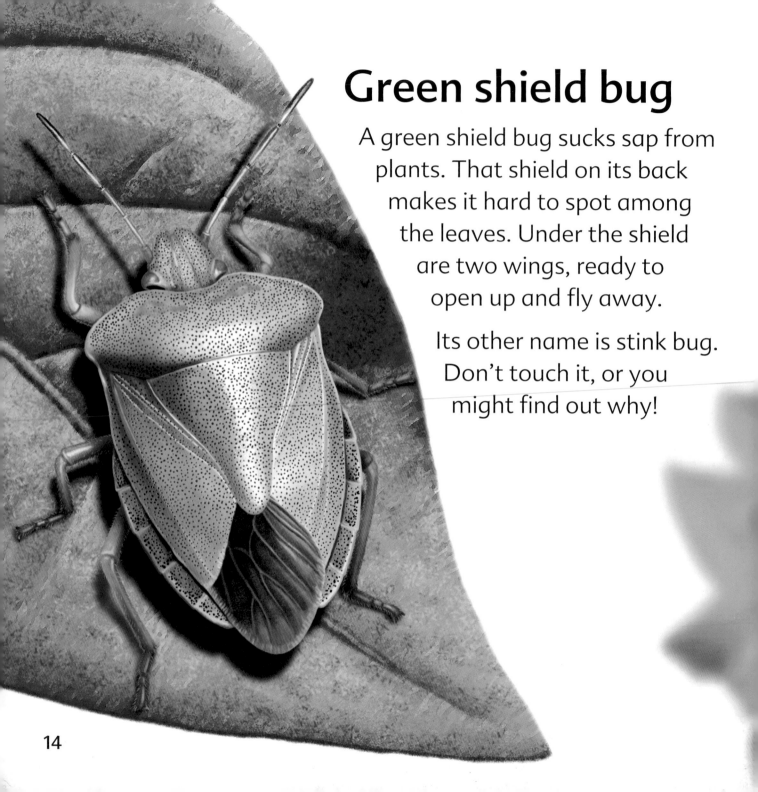

Green shield bug

A green shield bug sucks sap from plants. That shield on its back makes it hard to spot among the leaves. Under the shield are two wings, ready to open up and fly away.

Its other name is stink bug. Don't touch it, or you might find out why!

Who is it?

Something small is buzzing through the air.
It's round, red and shiny. Keep still.
It might land on you.

But what is it?

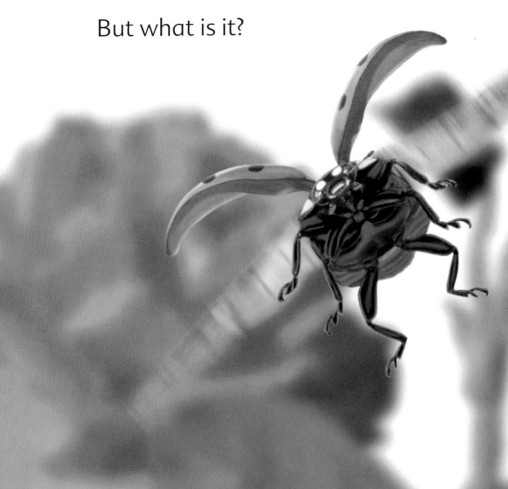

Ladybird

Did you know that a ladybird can fly? Underneath its shiny back are two folded wings. Count its spots when it lands. Some ladybirds have two, some have seven and some have 12, or even more.

How many spots can you see?

Who is it?

Something's hiding on the wall.

Can you see those wings peeking out? They look like scraps of old lace.

Who do you think they belong to?

Lacewing

It's easy to see how the lacewing gets its name. Look at the delicate, see-through patterns on its wings. These insects eat greenflies and other garden pests. In winter they often hide away inside our houses.

Who is it?

Has somebody been decorating this ragwort plant? There are tiny, colourful rings wrapped around the stems.

What do you think they are?

19

Cinnabar moth

Cinnabar moth caterpillars love to eat ragwort leaves. Their bright orange-and-black bands warn birds that they taste horrible. When these caterpillars grow up they turn into red-and-black cinnabar moths. You can see one on the plant behind. They fly by day and by night.

Who is it?

Zoom! Did you see that?
Two big eyes and a whirring rustle of wings.
It shot past just like a tiny helicopter.

Zoom! There it goes again.

But what is it?

Emperor dragonfly

It's an emperor dragonfly. When it lands you can see its long wings and colourful body. This big dragonfly is a fast flyer and a fierce hunter. It catches other insects in mid-air.

Don't worry! It's not big enough to eat you.

Who is it?

Boing! Something just sprang out when you walked through the grass. Did you see its long legs?

Boing! There it goes again.

What is it?

Grasshopper

It's a grasshopper. This insect is a champion jumper. Look how those long back legs are ready to spring. Grasshoppers live in long grass. Listen out for them in summer. Males chirp cheerfully by scraping their long legs against their wings. This brings females to listen.

24

Who is it?

Can you see two eyes on long stalks?
They are looking up, down and all around,
searching for a juicy leaf.

Who do you think they belong to?

Banded snail

It's a banded snail. That pretty pattern on its shell helps it to hide from predators. Each banded snail has a slightly different pattern. Some are yellow. Others are orange or white. Look out for them in overgrown places.

Who is it?

What's that little lumpy pile of earth on the lawn? It wasn't there yesterday. Something must have left it there.

But who?

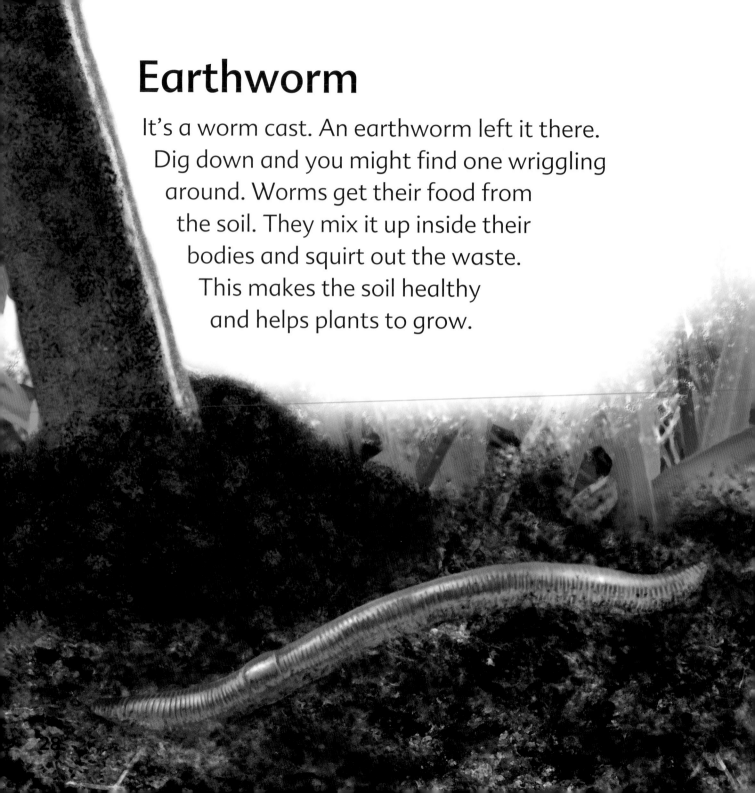

Earthworm

It's a worm cast. An earthworm left it there. Dig down and you might find one wriggling around. Worms get their food from the soil. They mix it up inside their bodies and squirt out the waste. This makes the soil healthy and helps plants to grow.

Who is it?

Watch out! Something is gnashing its pincers and waving its tail at you. It looks angry.

Poo! Now it's made a terrible stink.

But what can it be?

Devil's coach-horse

It's a devil's coach-horse. This fierce little beetle catches other small insects in its jaws.
When an enemy comes along it lifts up its tail to scare them away. If they come closer it squirts them with a stinky spray before running off.

Who is it?

Watch out!
There's a long, thin, black line snaking across your patio.

But look closer. That line is really lots of tiny insects.

What do you think they are?

31

Black garden ant

They're ants, of course!

These tiny insects are always busy.
The ones you can see are worker ants.
Their job is to collect food and build their nest
under the patio. Inside lives one queen ant.
Her job is to lay lots and lots of eggs.

Who is it?

Look at those long pincers.
They look just like a pair of tweezers.

Who do they belong to?

Common earwig

It's an earwig.
You often find these insects under stones.
Males have curved pincers and
females have straight ones.

Can you see the female carrying
her babies on her back? She
looks after them until they
are safe on their own.

Who is it?

Here's a tiny, shiny worm coiled up tight. But when it unwinds you can see lots of legs. So it can't be a worm after all.

What do you think it is?

35

Millipede

It's a millipede. It lives under logs and stones. See how its tiny legs move in waves. At the first sign of danger it curls up for protection. This millipede's body is made up of 50 segments with four legs on each.

How many legs does that make altogether?

Who is it?

Look. More minibeasts are hiding under this flowerpot. You can see their armoured backs, like tiny tanks. Those waving feelers help them get around in the darkness.

What do you think they are?

Woodlouse

They are woodlice. They live in damp, dark places, and feed on old, rotting plants.

Can you count seven pairs of legs?

This shows that woodlice are not insects. Crabs and shrimps are closer relatives.

Who is it?

Look at that shiny, silver trail.
It winds up, down and
all around the flowerpots.

But where does it lead?

Follow it and you might find out.

Black slug

A-ha! A big, black slug.

It's searching your garden for plants to eat.
Slugs don't have a shell to protect them,
like snails do. So they hide away under stones
and come out at night. This type of slug
comes in two different colours.

Can you see the orange one behind?
Don't touch, or you'll get sticky slime
all over your fingers.

Who is it?

Bzzzzzzz!

A bright, black-and-yellow insect
has landed on your picnic table.
It's looking for something
sweet to sip.

Don't panic.
Just stay still.
It will soon
buzz off.

But what
is it?

Common wasp

It's a common wasp. In spring wasps eat lots of pests, but in late summer they buzz around in search of sugary liquids to drink. They love juicy, rotten fruit — and your fizzy drink, too. That smart outfit is a warning. "Don't touch or I'll sting!" it says.

Don't worry. If you leave them alone, they'll leave you alone, too.

Who is it?

Legs, legs, everywhere!

Long and spindly, weak and wobbly, drifting on the breeze and bobbing across the lawn. Some have even landed on you.

But what are they?

43

Cranefly

They're daddy long-legs, of course.
Also called craneflies. Look closer.
They have a very long, thin body
and thin wings as well as their
famous legs. But that's
no problem. Craneflies
often lose a few legs.
It may even help them
to escape when a
hungry bird grabs
at them.

Who is it?

Oh dear!

One cranefly is stuck in a web. And something's coming. Something with long, stripy, hairy legs.

Better watch out, cranefly!

Garden spider

Too late. It's a garden spider, and it's come to gobble up the cranefly. Garden spiders spin a beautiful, circular web of silk. Then they coat it with sticky glue. Any insects that fly into the web get stuck fast. That's how the spider catches its breakfast.

Bug words

cast pile of waste soil left by a worm

chirp make a high, squeaky noise

nectar sugary liquid made by plants to attract insects

greenflies tiny green insects that damage some plants

markings patterns on any animal

relatives people related to you, such as your cousins

predator animal that hunts other animals for food

sap sticky juice that flows inside plants

segment small part

Find out more

If you have enjoyed this book and would like to find out more about minibeasts, you might like RSPB Wildlife Explorers.

Visit **www.rspb.org.uk/youth** to find lots of things to make and do, and to play brilliant wildlife games.

Index

48